DARK ROOMS:
A Saga

Siddharth Katragadda

PublishAmerica
Baltimore

© 2002 by Siddharth Katragadda.
All rights reserved. No part of this book may be reproduced in any form without written permission from the publishers, except by a reviewer who may quote brief passages in a review to be printed in a newspaper or magazine.

First printing

ISBN: 1-59129-503-3
PUBLISHED BY PUBLISHAMERICA BOOK PUBLISHERS
www.publishamerica.com
Baltimore

Printed in the United States of America

~ For my twin brother ~

Acknowledgments

I wish to thank several people. My mother, Rajini, for sharing with me her literary gene, her family history and her growing-up years. My father, Subrahmanyam, for constantly reminding me that my poems were worthy of the world. My brothers, Gopi and Shilpi, for pointing me in the right direction and for their comments of various drafts of this book. My wife, Kavitha, for her understanding. Sandy Chew for being my editor and for being my writing partner. Southern California Writer's Conference for workshops that changed the course of my writing career.

I would also like to thank the editors of the journals and anthologies in which these poems first appeared. I wish to thank the International Library of Poetry for their awards.

Finally, I would like to thank my homeland, India, for bringing poetry to my heart with its richness, and PublishAmerica for giving me an opportunity to bring this book to the world.

When a nation, a family, or a life faces upheaval, some revolt, while others give up and sit locked up within dark rooms, awaiting an end.

AUTHOR'S NOTE

All characters and events depicted in this book are fictional. The main characters were merely inspired by a family of six children who grew up in a house in some corner of old Hyderabad.

Notes:

The poems "The Bride Making," "The Bridegroom Making," "Reopening a Diary," and "The Mother-In-Law Making" first appeared on the online site Sulekha.com.

The poem "Beacon in the Wind" first appeared in "A Generation Defining Itself."

The poem "The Clock" first appeared on "Pigs & Poets."

The poems "A Boat on My Hand," "Birds of Carrion," "Pen, Paper and Ink," "The Cocoon," and "Ramdas of Golconda" first appeared in various International Library of Poetry anthologies.

Table of Contents

Part 1 – The Birth of Kaveri

Dark Rooms	17
A Lizard on the Wall	22
A Failed Generation	25
Bird in a Twister	29
The Shoulders of a Family	31
Mirabhai of Sai	33
Celluloid Naxalite	35
Meeting with Father	37
A Train in the Stomach	38
Either Goddesses or Prostitutes	40
Dancing on Bone	43
Kaveri	45
The Bazaar Girl	46
The Little Hindu	48
Surya	50
Gopal's Bell-Bottoms	53
The Blue Krishna	55
Holi with the Lord	57
Son of Fire	59
Ruins of Towli Chowki	62
This Sadness	64
The Foreign Car	66
Birds of Carrion	68
Ramdas of Golconda	71
Ten By Ten	72

Nine Lives	74
Tears in my Tea	76
Letting Kaveri Go	78

Part 2 – Monsoon of Kaveri

On My Acquaintances	83
The Taj's Poetry	85
Pen, Paper and Ink	86
How I Became a Poet	87
Rhapsody of Birds and Cows	90
Footprint in the Sand	92
You	94
The Worry Hanger	95
Of Organs, Frogs and Bees	96
God and Intelligence	98
Platforms of Yesterday's Trains	103
Cocoon	105
Eye of the Crossroads	106
A Boat on My Hand	107

Part 3 – Summer of Kaveri

Not a Sound to Hear	111
You Are the Country	113
The Country is in You	115
The Clock	117
A Lover's Recipe	119
Scaring Yama	121
A Knife in the Throat	123
Beacon in the Wind	125

My Mother's Sweat	126
The Mind's Impressionism	128
Will Work for Food	130
The Bride Making	132
The Bridegroom Making	134
The Reopening of a Diary	136
The Mother-In-Law Making	137
The Child Marriage	139
Poornima	141
The Dollar Seven Coats	143
The Passing of a Dream	144
Kaleidoscopes	145
Playing Yama	146
The Well	147
Tear in the Quarry	148
Kaveri's Last Summer	149
Stopping by Tank Bund	151

Part 1 – The Birth of Kaveri

Dark Rooms

In the study, now dark and deserted
The rusted gramophone tip
Lay stuck to the last track
Of the record, the drum to the side,
Like the head of its proud master
When death came to him,
One of those clear-blue summer
Afternoons in Hyderabad.
The music still echoed in the air,
Though it had been years
Since the voice of Shamshad Begum
Played in that room,
Lingering like a ghost that
Was determined to finish that unfinished song.
An invisible hand reached to crank the
Dead machine to life but slipped past.
The ghost of my grandfather,
Picking up his pen
The raven-colored India Ink in which
Had dried decades ago,
Tried to finish his unfinished book.
How painful it must be to die
And leave his characters unredeemed.
They were the ones who must have
Cried the most at his funeral.
They were the ones who must have
Pleaded for his resurrection,

Pledges that must have
Trapped him between worlds.

After all is said and done,
You stand and look at the walls,
The limestone-painted rooms,
The beds, with their large teak headboards,
The empty closets that a herd of lizards
Has made its home
The drama of a family unfold,
Where spiders tumble
On thin strings of silver saliva,
Where roaches scurry out at the
Sounds of the doors opening.
You try to tell yourself, like a confident shrink,
There has to be a reason.
If there has to be a cause, a reason for
Everything in this world then this is it.
These dark rooms are to blame.

This is probably where my grandfather
Hit the shivering head of his youngest son
For failing in math. Red marks were forbidden.
A place on the wall where the blue plaster
Had started to peel, revealing the fading white
Primer coat, and where still remained,
A silent reminder, a shallow dent
In the shape of a forehead.

In the middle room, full of clothes hangers
Without any clothes,
Like skeletons without bodies,
This was where my mother must have run
To get away from the wrath of her father
When his face became a marble effigy of contempt,

And his expression bordered on mockery,
His mouth straightened into a hard line,
When she earned less than full marks in Telugu class.
Her father's voice carrying over that of the mullah's,
Who screamed from the nearby Mosque,
Now where will she hide? Does she need to hide?
The object of her fright has turned into a ghost
Along with her secret hiding places.

Then, the kitchen. Where must have sat
My grandmother, her wicker rice sieve
Going "Shush! Shush!" as she prepared dinner,
The smell of cardamom and cloves in the air,
Fanning my grandfather,
While he voraciously swallowed his
Meals of oily, ghee-filled *pomfret* curry,
Feeding his brain than his stomach
Where his hungry characters
Could start playing their parts out.
Curry that was one day bound towards his heart
Like a pirate ship sailing to port.

From the kitchen opened the courtyard, where
My grandfather must have stood and listened
To the descent of his landlord's voice,
Words heaped in abuse,
Intermittent between sprinkles of saliva,
Showering down like mango-showers in mid-April,
About how much excess water they'd used,
How many months' rent had not been paid,
The words entering his veins, reaching his heart.

Fear, neglect and insult written in every corner,
On every wall. And pride, the worst of them,
Full of half promises, written everywhere.

On the front wall was a picture of grandfather,
Faded brown with age, tawny, sepia,
Standing proudly by his silver-gray Moris Minor,
One hand on the shiny hood,
The chrome glinting through his fingers,
His broad-carved face twisted in a proud smile,
And, had it not been a photo,
One could have seen a muscle flicking pompously in his jaw.
His firm mouth curled as if always on the edge of laughter,
His crooked nose giving him a kind of rugged geniality,
His hair, a cobweb of silver, light against his sun-whacked skin,
His expression darkened with an unreadable emotion,
Like a hunter who'd just skinned a man-eater alive.
Dressed in a whey silk shirt and khaki pantaloons, a sahib.
He had done his bar-at-law at Oxford.
Was the pride on his face bound to trickle
Into the minds of his young children?
Children, who, after he died, worshipped that picture
As piously as they did the many god pictures in the *puja* room.
Did it make them believe that pride alone
Would run their lives.
Like the Moris Minor that ran on
Petrol alone for many a year.
Chugging along, the wind in its domed windshield,
Kicking dust up in a swirl as it rattled past
Dusty village roads on the way to Gandipet Lake.
The lake shimmering smoother than snakeskin in the sun.
The fiery disc bisecting the horizon.
Dew-drenched grass glittering.
Past fields silver and green with ripening rice,
Six chattering kids sitting in the back, fighting over
Who sat near the windows, and who in the middle
So he or she could croon over their mother's head
In the front seat, and play with her sari gold-laced *pallu*.
And who sat on the father's lap and held the wheel.

DARK ROOMS

Each piece needed to be examined,
Like the innards of a mind.
Weighed for guilt. Interrogated.
Each room needed to be turned inside out,
Like Lord Narasimha, the half-lion, half-man, did
By splitting his foe in half with his bare hands.
I stood at the doorstep, neither indoors nor outdoors,
It was dusk, neither day nor night,
I am a shrink, neither a man nor animal.
I tried to invert this house, with all its dark rooms.
The failure of a life, or lives or a family
Or an entire generation lay in the environment that gave rise to it.
These dark rooms.

Notes:
    Mullah: a Muslim priest.
    Telugu: a Dravidian language spoken mainly in south-India.
    puja: prayer
    pallu: end of sari
    pomfret: type of fish
    Lord Narasimha: A man-lion avatar of Lord Vishnu who comes to earth to kill a powerful demon who could be killed neither indoors nor outdoors, neither during the day nor at night, and neither by human nor an animal.

A Lizard on the Wall

Gopal lay sprawled in one of the dark rooms,
The one that had the old paneled
Door open to the living room,
His face turned to one side.
His feet shook nervously, trying to wriggle
Out a lifetime of disappointments and letdowns
Through his trunk like legs, legs that stuck out
Through his polyester bell-bottom pants.
The radio aired a song from Mera Naam Joker
For the third time, that day, on the Vividh Bharati station,
On the old transistor that stood by his bed,
Sheathed in a leather case.

Avva, the maid, was late today, as usual.
His sleep had been interrupted periodically
In anticipation of her arrival.
He knew when she came, if she came,
By the sound of her sweeping the front patio.
Then, the tinkling of the steel vessels being cleaned,
The laundry being banged mercilessly on stone.
Then, the fragrance of simmering rice, mixed with
The smell of mutter frying in oil would lift in the air,
Coming to his nose in wafts, like the smell of his bride
Who came to him on their first night,
With niveous jasmine in her hair.

Thirty years ago, the Avva always came on time.

But that was back then, when his father,
The great writer, a pillar of Telugu literature, was alive.
And when all the children lived in the house.
Now, there was no one?
Just him, filling all those dark rooms,
Once noisy with cries of running children,
Playing with bows and arrows made from
Wet, algae ridden stalks from a broom
That the Avva used to clean the cesspool;
Or sticks pulled out from wicker curtains
That hung from the windows, leaving gaping holes in them.

One dark room for each one of them.
Dark rooms painted in watchet limestone,
Floors of deep-wine colored red-oxide,
More like curdled blood. Haematic.
A courtyard that opened to the cerulean skies,
And the cries of the upstairs people who
Yelled their water problems from the balcony.
In the kitchen, a huge grinding stone sat with a
Teak-colored wooden pound in it that had
Not been moved for ages since their mother used it,
Poised like a dancer stilled for life.
A sadness tied to each item, each room,
Like a talisman that wards off joy.

Who would make his lunch, today?
For three hours, he had been thinking of one thing.
Like anyone could think for that long about one thing.
What would he eat? Leftovers from two nights before,
A bitter-gourd fry that only he,
In his whole family, liked. Could ingest.
And some butter milk he
Bought from the Reddy Bros. Stores.

He watched a thick filemot lizard on the wall,
Just above the ceiling fan,
Which creaked at a pace slow enough for
Him to be able to look through its wings.
He wondered when the lizard would fall,
Whether the fan would catch it in its orbit,
Splattering it all over the ceiling.
What color is a lizard's blood, he wondered.
Red? Minium? Probably white.
It must have climbed in through the
Triangular hole in the glass ventilator window.
It had stood in the same place for two nights,
Moving only its tongue to catch unassuming prey.
How similar their lives were, he thought.

He should get up now, he thinks.
Food will not come to him, he
Would have to walk to the Mitai Bandar
On the main road and buy himself some son papdi.
He commanded his brain to awake but
It whirled in ever decreasing circles.
Why did he always wake up with the face of a bad night.
Pushing away the heavy clogging sleep, he struggled to sit up.
Now, a smile that dripped in sarcasm remained etched on his lips
As he looked at the lizard. He had won.

Notes:
    Mitai Bandar: Sweet Shop
    son papdi: Name of an Indian side dish
    Mera Naam Joker: Name of a Hindi movie

A Failed Generation

Each dark room, an undying
Reminder of a failed generation.
Three boys and three girls grew up in them,
Running and playing around their great father,
While he sat reciting poetry to
A young woman who came at five
Each morning, sat at his feet and
Wrote down his work, word for word.

Leela, the oldest, learning *bharatnatyam*
In the front room, churning her head and hips
Around like an uncontrollable top on a table.
Gopal and Krishna, the younger ones,
Chasing each other with broomstick bows and arrows,
Pretending to be Ram and Ravan. While Kamini,
The middle one, pretended to be Sita.
Gopal, held her by her oiled pigtails as
She ran to hide behind hangers of clothes.

Then, one day it happened.
A cyclone came out of the Bay of Bengal,
And turned their colorful house
Into a still black-and-white photo.
The only thing of color that remained was
The *paan*-red bougainvillea tree that
Grew along the compound wall
In a trellised canopy of smaragdine vines,

Its flowers, a splash of blood that had been
Stilled in time in its splatter, for eternity.

They were in the living room
When Ram, the oldest boy,
Onto whose shoulders the onus
Of their failed generation would fall,
Rushed into the room from his father's study,
His expression would remain
Stilled in all their memories
Like scenes from old Hindi films,
Like Raj and Nargis in the rain,
Under an umbrella, in Aawara,
Singing, *we have fallen in love,
Now why do we fear love*?
Like Madhubala's smile in Anarkali.
Black and white images that remain
For a lifetime, trapped in an organ
That washes off its images of all pigment
And retains no color.
What remains would fade with time.
Oh, whatever.
Importantly, they would never forget Ram's face.

But for little Ragini.
Too young to have memories,
Who remembered her father's face only
For his soft putty-clay like nose
That she could grab and play with.
Only two years of age, but who also cried
Not because of anything else but the
Fact that her mother left her,
Bare-bottomed on the cold floor.

"Some thing is wrong with father."
They all rushed to see what it was.
Their father lay on the floor,
His head on the rosewood desk,
A frown written between his eyes,
His pain carved in merciless lines on his face,

Evidence that his brain had acknowledged
The approach of death.
An inkpot dripped dark blue ink
Over its sides, onto the floor.
The gramophone tugged relentlessly
On the last track of a record,
The ending line of a film song
Repeating again and again in a voice
That seemed stretched like a rubber-band.

That single incident changed all their lives
At a time when they did not believe
That any single event in their lives
Could have such an altering effect.
The study was locked and bolted.
The rooms fell dark and silent.
Their mother, in the midst of six children,
Gave up living and sat by the window
Fanning herself in the summer heat,
Looking out of the meshed windows
At the rotting Moris Minor
That her husband used to drive,
Six children in the back,
To Gandipet, each weekend.

For two generations, their house had been a place
Where artists came and went at will,
Like flame-moths drawn to a kerosene lamp.

A rich, famous house.
Then, with one swish of the hand,
Everything disappeared and all
That was left were six children,
And a mother who willed not to live.
And a new generation was doomed to fail.

Notes:
    bharatnatyam: A traditional dance from South India
    Ram: Hindu deity, husband of Sita and prince of the state of Ayodhya.
    Ravan: Name of a Hindu demon who abducts Sita from Ram
    Sita: Ram's wife
    The song mentioned in this poem is from the Hindi movie *Awaara*

Bird in a Twister

The whole generation was doomed to fail,
Not just their family of six children.
An entire nation, caught in the maelstrom
Of a premature independence from the white Raj,
A colossal partition between two opposite faiths,
One saffron, the other green, the colors of the flag,
And the cataclysmic clash between
Emerging modernity and subdued values,
Struggled, like little birds caught in a twister.
Birds shot down to earth, burnt and smoldering
By crisscrossing lightening bolts.

Struggled in the dilemma between purpose and success,
At the crossroads between villages and towns,
And in the choices between religion and science.

The beautiful music of the veena was
Too subtle for ears that were, out of the blue,
Looking to follow the harsh drums of their hearts,
A dull noise that came from the west,
The desperate buzzing of a wasp trapped in a glass.

A nation of people were all doomed to fail,
Left to fend for themselves by a parent
That, having ruled their heads for three hundred years,
Decapitated those very heads and
Left their bodies stripped of all identity,

Left a people to squirm out to their newfound freedom
Like a newborn that squishes out, blood red,
Into its new world of problems and anticipation.
Like this family of six children would, when their father died.

Notes:
    veena: traditional Indian string instrument

The Shoulders of a Family

Ram, the oldest amongst the boys,
Wanted to follow his father and become a writer.
But dreams are for fools, and people without real problems.
How could he dream when
Five children cried to be looked after,
His mother dying. How could he dream when he awoke
To the drumming of water in shallow buckets and
The rumble of shallower tummies, each morning.

His dreams got enflamed in the midnight oil he
Burnt each night to become a doctor.
He moved to London and settled down there.
Years later, when his wife died,
Her cancer, starting in a breast, and eating hungrily
Into the pith of her soul, the sadness that would
Kill him emerged like bubbles in water
That come to the surface, float and burst, soundless.

His depression could not be cured
By his own hands even though he was the best shrink
In the whole of West London, though he treated other people
For maladies of the head.
It is easier to comprehend the pain of others than one's own.

He had given his best in trying to save their generation.
He came back to India, many years later, on a visit,
To find his property taken, property he built by forsaking his land,

Living in a depressed land where the winters bloomed
Dark and wet in his lonely heart.

His only other property, his heart,
Would become that of an Englishwoman,
Who tried to make him happy with her pale leucochroic breasts,
Each night, and promised to look after his two sons
As her own, but ended up watching him die.
His life slipping away from him with the one promise
He had awaited since he was twenty, the promise of tranquility.
A luteous golden eagle floating in the Himalayan skies.
The floating music of Lord Krishna's flute.
A house-boat moored on the shimmering Dal Lake,
Its reflection shaking like life, which was blurring in his vision.
He had failed his generation. The generation had failed him.
They were all doomed to fail.

Mirabhai of Sai

Wide-hipped Leela wanted to learn dance.
Her mom used to say that she had nice rounded buttocks,
Just the right amount of flesh in them for bharatnatyam.
But, like Ram, she learnt that dreams were dreams.
Churning one's backside to mrudangams
Does not run a life. Dancing to a husband's tunes runs a life.
Instead, she decided to leave. So, kid in hand,
She walked out into Hyderabad's monsoon,
One evening, the rain drumming against her face.
The wet winds feather-touched her with tantalizing persuasion,
Go on. Look for a new life outside these rains.
The sunshine broke across her face.

A new man entered her life. A married man!
But she did not care. Rebellious Kakatiya warrior blood
Ran in her veins. Incarnadine. The blood of fiercely
Brave Rani Rudramma, thinned by time-weakened genes.
Can logic alone rule a heart that begins to fall in love,
In a land just learning to love openly?
He gave her the children that would be symbols of their marriage.
They were her tali, symbols of her fertility,

She set up a press in her house and worked hard,
Each day, till perspiration ran between her breasts,
And her honey-colored skin glistened,
Printing wedding cards during the marriage season.
Wedding cards that reminded her of the wedding she never had.

At least not the wedding of her choice.
Mehndi-colored leaves in one corner.
A silver imprint of Lord Ganesha emblazoned,
The lord who removes obstacles.
The lord who always ignored her.
She made sure her cards always carried
With them the goodwill life never willed for her.

She would save enough for her daughter's dowry
So she could have a wonderful wedding.
No, she would not let her daughter find love.
She would marry a man of her choice.
In a way, she trusted only her taste in men,
She had not trusted her parents'.
And she would not trust her daughter's.

And then, after her responsibilities in life were over,
She would give up life and rest in the knowledge
That now, Sai Baba, the human-god, was all hers,
And she was all Sai's. His Mirabhai. He was her true love in life.

Notes:
    mrudangam: A traditional Indian percussion instrument
    Kakatiya: A kingdom that ruled the state of Andhra during the medieval times
    tali: A marital pendant
    Sai Baba: A holy man from the early twentieth century worshipped all over India.
    Mirabhai: A princess who gave up her royalty for an ascetic life in search of Lord Krishna

Celluloid Naxalite

Krishna, the youngest of all, would try to shirk failure, too,
And, like all his brothers and sisters, make a dash for success.
He had upper class, almost patrician features,
Devoid of any blemish that would bar his being called handsome
His features were so perfect, so handsome, that any more delicacy
Would have made him look womanly.

When still very young, he became an actor.
In his first movie, "Our Land," he acted as a young man
Who falls in love with a Lambadi woman,
Only to be taken in by Naxalites, Men of Mao Zedong,
Preaching violence, holding red communist flags and cheap country
Rifles that smoked fake gunpowder, singing revolutionary songs,
"We have tied bullock carts to carts.
Which cart are you coming in, O servant of the Nizam government.
Which cart are you coming in, O servant of the Nizam government."
He had the blood of a Kakatiya general in him,
That of Ganapati Rao, pure and red, after eight hundred years.

He dies in the end, shot by military police.
As a kid, when I watched him die,
I thought, quiet naively, he really died,
That I would never see him again. But I did, in this movie or that.
Women in bullock-carts sang to him, "Which cart are you coming
in,"

But he would not be taken in by any of them.
Life is full of bullock-carts. Some you catch. Others you miss.

Notes:
    Lambadi: A gypsy race found in certain areas of India, especially in Hyderabad
    Nizam: Rulers belonging to the Asif Jahi dynasty who ruled Hyderabad from 1724-1948 after the Moghul Empire collapsed.
    Naxalite: Left Wing Activist
    Mao Zedong: Chinese leader who inspired the Naxal movement
    The song mentioned in this poem is from the Telugu movie *Maa Bhoomi*

Meeting with Father

The water kooja in the kitchen had stood there for years.
It was the same kooja his father drank from when he was alive.
It had changed little in shape, color or function over all those years.
Probably a chip had fallen off the rim, here or there, that's all.

For Gopal, who was too young when his father died
To be able to have an intellectual conversation with his father,
This was a meeting ground.
He had seen the water ripple on occasion
As his hands went with the glass for a fill.
He was sure he had crossed hands with his father at the kooja.
They say dead souls need quenching, too, and this was where
The people who'd died in the house came for a fill.
In fact, they were the ones who cooled the water, he believed.
Which magician was behind all this? Why did the water level fall?
In the hot, windless nights? The science of evaporation
Was not known to him. He just stood there and
Talked away to the walls, watching the water in the pot shake,
The hair on his hands standing.

Notes:
kooja: A pot

A Train in the Stomach

On the blood-red oxide floors
He thought he saw the impression of a footprint,
Five toes and the rounded sole,
Separated by the high arch in his father's feet.
The one footprint that got away, perhaps.
Avva's thick coconut-stick broom
Could not sweep it under the beds.
His father must have stood there
When the bloody ache spread through his veins.
He must have calmed his heart
By focusing his mind on Savitri
His rotund-bottomed, papaya-breasted character,
Walking away to a happier place with her,
Dodging his heart with just thought.

Gopal Mama's stomach rumbled
Like it did on many an occasion
When he went empty-stomached to the radio-station.
The whole nation, tuned to *Vividh Bharati*,
Must have heard his stomach fill up
With butterflies, hungry ones.

You can shoo away a heart attack
Suppress a yawn, hold off an incipient erection, even,
By focusing your attention on the ugly eunuch
By the street corner that lifted her sari, proudly,

Up for the world to notice her duality.
But you can never stop an empty stomach
From whispering its secret wants.

Notes:
    Vividh Bharati: Indian Radio Station

Either Goddesses or Prostitutes

When my mother was in college she rode
The morning bus, 61 to Osmania,
With her classmates, all girls, of course,
In the bleak early moments of sunrise.
The love laws had been well in place in the city,
Strengthened by generations of Moslem presence.

There are two types of women. No in-betweens.
Firmly defined primaries. Well-partitioned primitives.
Like blacks and whites, without the grays of blurry eyes.
Like joys and sadness, without the ascetic calm.
Like ups and downs without plateaus.
The girls of god—fair, bejeweled, virtuous,
And the girls of Satan—dark, plain, shameless.

If your sari *pallu* covered both breasts
While you rode on the bus, you were prayed to as
A version of Goddess Laxmi.
If the same cloth slipped under the open V
Of the neckline, you were brazen. Spoilt. Provoking.
If either breast escaped into the world of prying eyes,
You were the prostitute of society. Scum. Poison.
Amazing how the lateral movement of a
Single piece if cloth could define
The morality of a human being.

Surprising, even, that the same men,
The men who wrote those unwritten laws,
Waited for the woman in front to
Turn from a goddess into a prostitute.
Goddesses were for *puja* rooms.
Did goddesses bring the scent of lust to their souls,
Fresh, ripe jacinthe *chameli* wrapped around one hand,
Whiffing it across their noses, bangles clicking,
Bringing blood to their phalluses,
Inciting that wonderful heat in their loins.

My mother was a goddess.
Some man tried to bring her down from her pedestal.
For the thrill was in watching the
Delight of a demon mixed in the shame of divinity.
A blob of scum on the fresh petals of a new flower.
He moved close to her, rubbing his chest against her back.
She glared at him and he smiled back,
Enjoying the scare in her eye,
Watching the embarrassment linger in her pupils.
The long deep look they exchanged infuriated her.
The smile in his eyes contained a mocking sensuous flame.
Their eyes locked in open warfare.
His practiced masculine eye took in every detail.
Smelling the jasmine in her hair,
Tied around the bun of her hair.
He rubbed his lips against her back
That stuck out, proud and strong,
Through the back of her nylon blouse.

It was quick and transient.
The bus lurched to a stop at Hari Bowli,
The fog of smoke and dust entering through the
Windows, blurring her vision like a cataract.
The man got out, quietly, through the ladies door

Before she even felt the wetness of the saliva
He left on her shoulder, where his lips had touched her,
The smell of a Charminar cigarette in it.
The mark of initiation. She was now a girl of Satan.

Notes:
    Osmania: name of a University
    Laxmi: Goddess of wealth
    puja: prayer
    chameli: a flower

Dancing on Bone

Yadagiri, an old friend of Gopal Mama's
Came to visit him one day, when I was a kid,
Yadagiri saw me and took me in his arms.
He had always been fond of me.

Gopal Mama, heard the dull thud of the bolt
On the high gate outside, pulled himself off
The bed and came out onto the patio.
I am sad today, Yadagiri, he said,
Will you do your *tandav* dance for me?

Yadagiri, a dancer, had learnt the *bharathnatyam*.
He started dancing on the patio with me in his arms
Moving to the music in his head
To *tublas* that drummed ceremoniously
With the beat of his heart, scarcely reaching his ear.

He moved to the wind in his lungs.
Krishna is playing his flute to cows.
He trembled on the strings of the *veena*
That cut through to the bone.

He faltered, and it stopped.
What would happen if Shiva, Lord of dance,
Faltered in his cosmic dance, he thinks,
Would you and I be here?

He moved on, afraid as he had been
All his life, of the smallest things
Like he is now of stopping and
Never again hearing that song.

Notes:
    Krishna: Hindu deity of love
    Shiva: Hindu deity, the destroyer.
    tandav: Lord Shiva's Nataraj pose
    tubla: Traditional Indian percussion instrument
    veena: Traditional Indian string instrument

Kaveri

"Kaveri,
Where can I find you?"
Gopal Mama said that he was sad
Because he reminisced about Kaveri.
He had been divorced to her
For twenty years, now.
She remarried, moved to the United States,
Married a professor, had two rackety kids,
Lived happily ever after.
Life was not full of such
Fairy tale endings for him.

"Kaveri,
Where can I find you.
In the water that bathes my body,
In the teardrops that cleanses my soul,
In the rivers that quench my thirst,
Or the sweat that emerges from me
As rewards of my tribulations,
To come back to me as rain.
Kaveri, where can
I find you."

Notes:
    Kaveri: name of a river in south India

The Bazaar Girl

Gopal Mama rarely goes out.
He goes out only to sing—to Lad Bazaar—
The Street of Love, rows of glittering bangle shops,
Built for Ladli Begum by the Sixth Nizam.

He sings to himself, uncaring of the unnoticing people
Who walk past him as though
They did not want to loan him their lips,
A smile in applause of his dry, lifeless song.

He searches for the inspiration that deserted his lines,
The bazaar girl who once window-shopped,
Each evening, on the street where he sat singing. Kaveri.

She capered buoyantly on the words of his songs,
Smiling softly, as she tried on multicolored bangles
On her peach-colored hands.
Bangles that shone and sparkled like the
Bright stars, displayed like jewels, in the stelliferous skies

One day, she eyed him with startled interest
When she noticed he was watching her.
As their eyes met, he felt a shock run through him.
Now, they were eyeing each other like two bantam cocks.
A probing query came into his eyes,
An invitation buried in the smoldering depths.
He gave her a quick conspiratorial wink.

Thought he detected a flicker in her melanic intense eyes.

Her participation contained an intimacy she hadn't intended.
Then, she turned her gaze, embarrassed,
Conscious suddenly of his evil intent.

Surprisingly, from then on, she made no attempt to hide
The fact that he was watching her.
She even leered at him slyly,
Meeting his half glances with hers.
She tipped him only with her smiles,
Not cold coins in the colder winters,
Nor pocket-warmed coins in the simmering summers.

He searches for that sinewy arm that holds concealed a red iron,
Covert in the color of her blood, a chauvinistic phallus
Buried in the fountainhead of her smiles,

"Her man won't let her out, Her man won't let her out,"
Waiting for Kaveri in the *bazaar*, the essence of his songs and
The pretense for his living, he sings in Gol Boli to the Lambadinis,
"You are not visible to my eye, just like these burka-clad women
Who come to this bridal *bazaar* during the month of Ramadhan."

Notes:
    bazaar: market
    burka: A feminine Muslim outer-garb
    Ramadhan: Muslim festival

The Little Hindu

Yadagiri brawled with a Muslim man
On his way to Kachiguda,
The vein in his forehead swelling like
A thick, black snake, anger flickering in his eyes,
We, plant-eating, forbearing,
Weakling Hindus have survived you,
Though you slaughtered us in
Mountains you called "Slaughter of Hindus"
He did not like them very much,
The Nizam folk of Hyderabad,
He was always picking up fights with them.

To Yadagiri's tantrums on religion,
Gopal Mama replied, "Who am I to talk about religion.
I am just a little Hindu. So little,
My palms scarce grace each
Other in prayer, nor my knees the ground."

"I have stopped going to the temple next door,
Built in the tiny space between compound walls.
A spiked metal gate opens to the temple.
A dried lemon, dotted with *tantric* symbols, hangs over it.
The goddess Kali, with a fan of arms around her,
Beckons me from within. Not one man has come to
See her, in this, the *Age of Kali*."

"But I rarely go. Even when I do,
I seldom genuflect in front of her
Rarely pour my tears at her feet
In overpowered deluges of sorrow.
Rarely has my brow been blessed with her blood
Churned in nacarat vermilion,
My hair by coconut flavored juice
Tasted by her, mixed with her saliva.
Rarely have I lifted up on a toe
To ring her bell, to hear her voice in its clanging."

"So small am I, she, so *Big*, built out of
And into the pith of every man's cerebration.
Yet, my hauteur annuls any little need
That may exist to lean a little onto her,
To reveal a little of the soul.
Trotting a lonely road am I,
A road where no temple gates face my direction.
And all seven doors of the *seven-hill Lord*
Remain shut to me. Shelter less. On I go, with little ado.
A little Hindu."

Notes:
    tantric: having to do with Tantra
    Kali: Hindu Goddess
    seven-hill Lord: Lord Venkateshwara
    Hindukush: A mountain range in Afghanistan believed to be a
    place of genocide of Hindus.

Surya

Surya, an odd-job artist who drew cartoons
For local Telugu periodicals,
Knocked on the gate. A bag over his shoulder,
His hair uncombed (for it was wavy
And never needed combing),
He looked just like an artist.

His eyes smarted as he tried to accustom them
To the dark rooms after the bright sun outside.
Oh, all the artists of Kachiguda are here, he said,
Seeing Gopal and Yadagiri.
The waste product of society.
His homely face rearranged itself into a grin.
Let's drink to that. He showed off a
Bottle of Chivas Regal he'd bought at the
Local liquor store with the money
From one of his recent cartoons.

"You, Yadagiri, can dance better
Than Nutan or Meena Kumari.
But who will come to see you?
No one. They all want to see Helen
Grind her ass to the tune of Mehbooba.

And you, Gopal? You sit and arrange words
All day long in closed dark rooms

DARK ROOMS

The darkest of them being the inside of your head,
As dark as the hair on your head,
As dark as your raven skin.
Why, you must be Krishna, the lord of love, the ebony one.
Nigrine.

And I. I drew a self-portrait today
Of my own face by looking in a mirror.
An artist tries his best to make
His subject appear presentable on canvas.
He curls straight eyebrows,
He specks an unadorned cheek with a beauty spot.
He sculpts flat bottoms into big round *koojas*,
He shapes slit-eyes into big almonds,
Like the ones used in preparing *qubaani ka meetha*.
But how could I make this face,
This horrible face, a face scarier
Than that of the villain Pran's,
On which small pox has licked large pocks,
How can I make this face look beautiful?
So I sit and draw beautiful
Doll-like Bapu's pictures of women,
Women with pot-like buttocks,
Papaya-like breasts and peacock-like features.

We are all the waste products of society.
There is little value in this world
For my face,
Or your words, Gopal.
Or your *nritya*, Yadagiri.
Let's drink to that."

With that, they came towards me,
Pushed me to the ground and opened my mouth.

The pungent smell of alcohol filled my mouth.
Thu, thu, I spat, like petrol had been poured down me
While they sat around, laughing.

Notes:
    qubaani ka meetha: Indian sweet dish
    nritya: dance
    kooja: round pot
    Pran: Hindi film villain
    Bapu: famous Indian artist

Gopal's Bell-Bottoms

Surya looked at Gopal Mama's bell-bottom pants
And said, "What Gopal, you are still wearing those pants
The world is changing so fast.
The seventies have come and gone and you are still the same."

Gopal Mama looked at his pants defensively,
His eyes flashed in a familiar display of impatience.
Brushing his now archaic step-cut styled hair off his face,
He tried to clean the steam off his glasses.
What is the use in changing?
The past has always proved me a fool.
Today, they wear blue colored khadi that has come
In from the west. Gandhi's wheel has fallen silent.
Tomorrow, time will laugh at these, too, so why change.

Gopal Mama still listened to those sad, melancholy-dripping
Songs from the old Hindi movie, *Devdas,*
"When the heart is broken, what will I get by crying?"
"When the heart is broken, what will I get by crying?"
Time can make you forget old sadness,
Even send it back in the guise of new happiness,
But will sadness go away from people's hearts.
Will the meaning of it change just because
A new happiness is now in fashion.
Women these days walk around showing their bosoms,
Their breasts spilling out of their blouses.

It is in fashion but can fashion alone hide the pain in their hearts.
The past has always proved me a fool.
The past has always proved me a fool.

Notes:
    Devdas: Hindi film about a man who drinks himself to death after losing his lover. The song mentioned in this poem is from this film.

The Blue Krishna

As kids, my bothers, cousins and I would
Climb to the top of the green high-gate and
Use the bolt to grind seed with.
Thud, thud.
What we used the seed for, I don't quite remember,
It is too far back to go back and fetch,
Something so trivial. What is not trivial,
Something so permanent in the mind's eye,
Something I would never have to go back for
Is the other side of the compound wall,
Visible only from atop the gate

One day, we got to the top,
Our knees scratched by nails in the wood,
And looked to the other side.
Nothing stirred there, but for a blue mynah
That sat on the carefully laid garden
And cooed some nature-orchestrated song
To the hot, windless summer afternoon.
A fountain stood in the middle of the garden,
Dried up, covered in leaf-green algae,
Shriveled creepers crawling over it.
A statue of Lord Krishna stood in the middle,
Playing his flute to invisible cows
That seemed to materialize in our vision,
A soft song rising in the air.
He had skin the color of the cloudless

Azure depths of the skies above.
Wasn't he a dark boy? Why the blue?
Was it euphemism, in a land where
To have dark skin was to be
A sinner in a previous life,
A way of repaying the curses of your karma.
The unmoving smile etched on Krishna's face

Lit up in our eyes, as we watched.
The fountain sprung to life around the statue.
We fell back, onto the patio.

Holi with the Lord

On *holi* day, when we tired ourselves by
Spraying color-water on each other, all morning,
Till our bodies glimmered in all shades of
Safranine, chalcedonic, rosy twilights and slategreen,
And our shirts clung to our bodies,
Our privates, wet and cold from the dampness,
Multicolored, for that was where the colors collected,
We had an idea.

We climbed the gate. Got onto the other side.
Lord Krishna watched us, still.
We rubbed color into the palms of our hands
And approached the Lord, our hearts beating
Like Shiva's *dholak* in our chests.
We aimed our plungers,
Our water pistols filled with colored water.
Four feet from him, distance enough for our
Young feet, if we needed to scoot,
We let out a scream and shot our pistols.
The colored water hit the Lord's face,
The blue of his skin melting down his body,
Mixing with the yellow, red and green.
In our vision his smile vanished,
Wiped away by astonishment,
Then, it reemerged and regained its stagnancy.
We danced and pranced around the statue,
Clapping our hands joyfully,

A silent fear building in our hearts.
What if Lord Krishna cursed us for this crime?
What if he sent his *chakra* flying that very moment
To remove our sinful heads?
What if we, like him, were cursed with dark skin
In our next lives?

Notes:
    holi: festival of color
    dholak: Traditional Indian percussion instrument
    chakra: A disk with serrations

Son of Fire

God and race were put in my
Head at a very early age.
One day, my mother burnt her
Hand while cooking murukku,
The dough snaking out of the plunger
And landing in the oil with a swoosh.
The oil danced up and down
Like jittery fish in hot water,
Splattering out of the *bandli*
And onto her fair hands.
She came and showed me the consequences,
Vermeil blisters, the color of her bridal ruby bangles

Look, she said, this is how you
Burn your hands in life.
But you – you have come out of Agni.
You can never be burnt by anything. Anyone.
You have the boiling red blood
Of Rani Rudramma in your virescent-green veins.
Fire does not burn fire.
It creates more fire, renews its strength.
It creates sparks that will glow in you
When the dusk disappears into inky ash,
Like goldenrod baby rockets that trace the skies
During the darkest nights of Deepavali.

The monsoon showed its face,
Unleashing a silver spear
That traced its way across
The melanic sky like a silver Boeing.
My mother took me in her arms and
Sat me on her lap.
Watching the rain lashing across the open balcony,
The trees swaying in the vapory downpour,
She said, no rain shall put the fire in you out.
No wind can simmer your many arms,
No sun can shine brighter than you.
The son of the fire-god, Agni, you are.
Surya, Vayu and Indra all respect your might.
Dressed in black, you will be.
You will have four hands, a javelin in one.
A chariot drawn by red horses, you will ride,
As the true blaze of sunrise arises
Above the last vestiges of night

Covering my face with her sari *pallu*,
She looked me in the eye,
The fire in you has no source.
It is not a river that comes from the ground.
Nor does it arise from wood, coal or paper,
The inflammables.
Without a birth, a cause, it exists.

You will burn many hearts when you are grown.
As a moth comes uninvited to a flare,
Women will flock around your warmth
Flutter, lick you, taste you,
And die in their lust around you,
Their tongues burnt the color of earthworm-purple.
As will your enemies, singed by your blue heat.

The bearer of the flammeous Kakatiya torch, you are.
Across generations, this flare goes with you,
As it has for centuries.
The light of our race rests in you.

Go out on your red horses when you are grown
And form your own army,
As did the brave generals of the Kakatiyas.
The Kaktiyas, who fought for us with their lives,
Giving a name, a tongue and an identity to us tribal folk.

Notes:
    murukku: Indian side dish
    bandli: a deep pan
    Agni: Fire god
    Surya: Sun god
    Vayu: Wind god
    Indra: Rain god
    pallu: End of a sari that wraps over the woman's bosom
    Rani Rudramma: medieval queen of Kakatiya dynasty

Ruins of Towli Chowki

As kids, we often went to Towli Chowki,
A suburb just below the hill fort of Golconda,
Here, the Qutb Shahi tombs lined the horizon
Like sentinels of a past dynasty.
The sunset often loomed like a sheath of flame

We stoned down dates from the tops
Of palm trees that lined Ragini Pinni's farm.
Climbed Tamarind trees to pluck the burnet-ripe, sour fruit.
Scavenged for beaver-bird nests
With little albicant-white eggs in them, unhatched,
That we thought we were saving
From some unknown enemy.
Yes, we were saviors of the world,
Little brats, dressed in little shirts and khaki shorts.

The ruins stood just outside the farm wall.
The domes had long since given way.
The arched windows were crawling with creepers
Inside, stone steps led down to a derelict bath,
Unused since god-knows-when,
Filled with corbeau, algae-stinky water.
We cupped little, black tadpoles in those dirty waters,
Brought them back home and kept them
In empty pickle bottles thinking they were fish,
And watched them die, their tummies turned upside-down.

Once, on one of our many visits,
Ragini Pinni's two sons, my cousins,
Fell in the pool. I watched their black heads
Disappear below the virid waters,
Surrounded at once by a shoal of tadpoles.
I put my hands in and pulled them both up
By their shirt collars. They emerged, spitting green water.

We know why the fish are dying,
They told me in the evening, after they
Finished getting their share of scolding from
Ragini Pinni for going to that *bhooth* bungalow.
The ghost of Quli Qutb Shahi's begum roams there,
She warned them. They went on in hushed voices,
We know how it felt to be in their world.

My mother took me in my arms,
Proud I had saved my cousins.
You are the keeper of the universe, she said,
You were born to save lives.
A silent conviction creeping into her heart
Accentuated by the heave of her proud breast.

Notes:
    Bhooth: Ghost

This Sadness

Let's not talk of religion today, Yadagiri,
He said, *what good is religion*
To a man who has nothing but dark rooms
And a sadness that lasts a lifetime.
Can religion alone cure this retrophile.
For an instant, a wistfulness
Stole into his emotionless expression.
When he lifted his eyes,
The pain still flickered coccineous there.
"This sadness creeps up my spine,
Reaching its long lost gratification
In the oasis of my heart."

Gopal Mama remembered his father's face,
Blue and ashen, lying in a pool of blue ink,
As blue as his blood. The blood of his characters.
His big belief in life was he would die the same way,
His heavy, burdened heart would give way,
Explode in his chest like his father's did,
And no one would even know he died.
Then, the blue stench of death would ride
Up the open shaft of the courtyard.
The upstairs people would come running,
More worried about the rent he had not paid
For the last three months, than his health.

"Pumping against the banks and
Numbing every sand on the sides,
Moving like the Lucifer, riding my life-stream.
An omen of insanity, traveling
To the pith of my thoughts.
Numbing my rationalism in its course,
Calling in with it, dark clouds of distrust
And gales of suspicion"

What was Gopal Mama suspicious of?
Kaveri left him years ago,
She did not remarry without his consent.
She did nothing behind his back.
"It finds its strength in a telling blow.
Its clenched fist breaks through my heart's sinews,
Buried to the wrists in my blood-drenched soul.
Then, breaking free like
A dying parasite off a dead host,
It trumpets off to find salvation in another soul."

The Foreign Car

One day, sitting in the front verandah,
Gopal's lazy head on her lap, her fingers
Tracing the edge of his dark, unpleasant face,
Kaveri looked at the picture of his father,
Standing next to the Moris Minor,
And said, "Where is your father's motor, now."
Oh, sold long ago, he answered, his eyes closed.
It was a foreign car, you know, he boasted.
Her eyes lit up. *A foreign car?*
She looked down at him through the curtain of hair
That had fallen loose from her plait

I want to have a foreign car, one day, she said.
And he laughed, his teeth yellow in the dark.
Those days were different, he explained,
Now, who has foreign cars? The age of the Raj is over.
If you want a foreign car, you have to go to 'foreign.'
As though foreign was the name of a place.
Crestfallen, her smile quickly faded.
Then, a devilish look came into her eyes.
An idea creeping into her mind like a cockroach snuggling into a shoe,
Like flavescent moonlit mist entering a room in winter,
Like the wisps of *holi* color, floating in the winds of April.
Two dimples emerged, as if loving fingers had squeezed her cheek.
A soft curve touched her lips. She took on a solemn glow.
Somewhere, a shadow lurked in the back of her mind

A smile struggled its way through the mask of uncertainty.
Something grew coldly determined inside of her.
With a soft sigh, she settled her mouth on his.

Notes:
    holi: Indian festival of color

Birds of Carrion

Gopal Mama tried to explain to Kaveri,
One monsoon evening. Sitting in the patio,
The rain falling on the concrete floor,
Seeping up the bottom of her sari,
Flowing down her lotus feet,
Collecting in little drops on her petal-pink toes.
She was watching the huge wooden gate
With a heavy iron bolt.
Her face was firmly set in deep thought,
Wondering when she would get out of that gate,
As though the gate were a dam.
Kaveri is the name of a river
In south India that dries up in summer,
But runs free and full after the monsoon rains
Have come and left the air smelling of earth.
Wondering when she could leave.
This house, with all its dark,
Limestone-painted rooms,
Was not what she expected out of life.

She surveyed herself critically in a
Polished metal hand mirror.
She hued her lips with just enough puniceous lipstick
To show that her mouth was perfect.
She worked irately at a tangle in
Her hair with the ivory comb

She was not as beautiful, anymore, she thought,
No longer a picture of feminine certainty.
A badly preserved twenty-nine.
Her face retained only traces of youth.
Her prettiness was utterly commonplace, now,
Her eyes sunk in the pallid hollow of her face
But she was still too good-looking for Gopal.

Her only friend, the sari man, came each month
With a bundle of saris, tied up in a white cloth,
Lighting her eyes up with saris of chiffon and organdy,
Hued in parrot-greens and lotus-pinks dyes.
Or sheer nylon-polyesters ones
Printed with purpureal primroses,
The same print and color a popular heroine wore
In one of the latest hit films
Running at Deepak Mahal Talkies.
And Venkatagiri silks, with gold-laced borders,
That came from the holy city of Tirupathi.
Fit only for goddesses like her to wear.
In his very own words, "If you wear this,
People will not be able to take their eyes of you.
No woman would be able to stand up to you."
"Where will I wear them, Venkatgaru?" she complained,
"He does not take me anywhere."
"I will not blame the poor man.

He has such a desirable young bride,"
He said, clicking his tongue,
Then he added, "You are taking this, are you not?"
"This is the last time!" she warned him, angrily,
"Don't come back till *Deepavali*."
You cannot keep me still, Gopal, she told him that day.
She glanced up at him under her eyelashes.
I am a river. I need to flow. If you try to stop a river,

It kills the people around it.
Surprise siphoned the blood from Gopal Mama's face.
He smiled benignly, as if dealing with a temperamental child.
He dropped his lashes quickly to hide the hurt

He answered, "Where lies understanding?
We're two different persons.
Why can't we see—the birds of carrion
Have often whispered in the ears of God,
You make the kill, dear lord,
And we'll keep your backyards clean.
The bone in your finger is just a ceramic.
The brain in your head, a bloody sponge.
Till they got together and built
All the bridges in the world;
The heaven-seeking minarets of Charminar;
The embroidered domes of the Qutb Shahi Tombs;
The rich durbars of the Golconda Fort.
Were these built without understanding between tissues.
So, my Kaveri, you should ask not
Of where understanding lies,
Or where it comes from, but where it meets."

Notes:
    Deepavali: Festival of lights

Ramdas of Golconda

"In every one of us sings a minstrel,"
Gopal Mama said to Yadagiri, looking at the limestone walls,
At the green moss where the rain water ran down,
"He sings a sad song of his many long years in
Confinements of incredulity. He strives in vain to get a release
From manacles that bind his emotions in prisons of distrust.

Like Ramdas, jailed in a dark dungeon in Golconda Fort,
Caught for embezzling moneys for his lord.
Whose songs fall on the deaf ears of the great Qutb Shah,
Who sits atop the hill watching Taramati
Sing boring love songs from her pavilion on the plains below.
His songs were never meant for mortals, anyway,
They were created for the ears of god, alone.

He wants to escape into that land of thought
Where a voice that comes from the bottom of the heart
Is not confused as a groan from hell.
There's no place for such a song till long after your day has come.
Then the minstrel will sing louder, many a blanched ear will then hear,
Of how you came and how you went."

Ten By Ten

"For twenty years I've been here.
This ten by ten forms my world.
This dark room, which has not
Seen the sight of open daylight.
At first, I used to spend hours gazing
Through the bars that run across these windows.
Hours peering through the holes
In the green wicker curtains
Where we pulled the sticks out,
As children, to make bows and arrows.
Once in a while, I used to cock an eye
Out of the window at the clouds

But now, after all these years
I hardly look beyond them.
For me, that space has ceased to exist.
Space is not around you but in your mind.
Really. Really.
The bones in my body, hinged to another
In a veneer of skin, unable to move
But in one translation or another,
So are my thoughts about the outside.
I hear that it is a bigger prison, out there,
Of people jailed to their cycles,
Of bosses at work, signals at a crossing.
I think I'm better off here than the world outside.

At least, I have owned my space,
Never mind, it's only a ten by ten."

Nine Lives

"For a whole year he put up with me.
Raja, my grayish-black, cat-eyed
Splendidly muscled cat.
That's probably ten in his.

After Kaveri left me and went away,
Only he stayed back. He had his own dark room,
The space between my arms and my neck.
A long time to remain incarcerated
In my uncomforting hands, my incessant adoring.

He hid from me, one day, behind the dresser.
The next day, he vanished.
I never saw him again. He'd move on.
Some speeding van trampled him, perhaps.
Maybe he framed his disappearing act,
His own silent felicide
So I wouldn't think he left me. Like Kaveri did.

I cried for him that day
As I did for few people in my life.
Not even for Kaveri, when she left.

They say a cat has nine lives. Short ones.
How do you live through nine lives, dear one,
When I find one life so hard to get by.

They say a cat moves as many homes.
If you should run out of houses in the neighborhood,
Or should come back in another proud birth,
I sure would like to meet. I sure have missed you."

Tears in my Tea

Gopal Mama watched her approach,
Her anklets jingling softly.
The bed, covered in rose petals, rubious,
The color of her lips. Lips that quivered
Under her sari *pallu* as she sat down,
A glass of *badam-flavored* milk in her shy hands.
Her red-green bridal bangles
Clanged against each other,
Awakening his manhood, like bells
At the temple that awaken the gods.

He took a teaspoon in one hand
And stirred dreams into her eyes.
Evoking memories that she has to leave behind.
He watched them mix in with her tears.
Her tears, like the milk,
Niveous and transparent at inception
Were now bursting with colorful thought.
Like his tea, now the color of her nipples
When he primped them with his fingers.

Filled with a new anticipation, a quiet fear
Causing a secret wetness between her legs,
She turned away, the sound of a smile escaping her,
The sound of moist lips parting.
He drank from her eyes to his heart's content.

DARK ROOMS

Only the heightened color of her cheeks
Betrayed her inner turmoil
As red flew to her cheeks.
The dim table light lit the edges of her hair.
He pushed stray tendrils away from her cheek.
Bending forward to get a glimpse of cleavage,
He nibbled her ears. A Gynotikolobomassophile.
His hand, gently insistent, moved slowly
Over her forehead and down her temples.

Her fingers moved across the smooth
Sweat-slippery flesh of his back.
Pleasure softened his granite-like face.
His lips continued to explore her soft ivory flesh
That left her skin feeling drawn and tight.
She pushed him away. He fought her resisting hands.
His eyes sparkled with the love of combat.
Her heart hammered against his ribs.
Her breasts tingling against his hair-roughened chest.
He assumed the superior position.
Suddenly, she realized that she had closed her eyes,
Giving in to the temptation of sleep.
The butterfly of his fingers searched for her nipples.
Her lashes swept down across her cheekbones
And she fell asleep in his arms,
A small sound of wonder came from her throat,
The piston-driving strength of his body possessing her dreams,
As he entered her, a nipple in his mouth.
Her breath still came in long, surrendering moans,
Until the man-heat had vanished, and a soft pain remained.

Notes:
badam: nut

Letting Kaveri Go

Letting Kaveri go was difficult for Gopal Mama.
He would tell her when she spoke of leaving,
An almost imperceptible note of pleading in his voice,
An expression of innocent childish imploring on his face.

"The unborn child curses the walls
That surround it, straitjacketing
It in its gravid prison."

"The naive fish scowls profanity
At its world of resistance
And seeks its place in the realm of air."

"Where does the newborn featherling,
Its wings as soft as jelly,
Go in the freedom of the skies."

"What should I do when you cry,
Like that lungless fish and the wingless young bird,
For a release from my heart."
His voice was heavy with irony.
He gave her a look of withering contempt.
A look of sadness passed over her features.
He saw an almost painful sympathy in her eyes
He deliberately exaggerated the pain in his face.

Kaveri did leave him and go.
A moth-wing flutter of her hand
Sketching a farewell wave, *bye*,
And she was gone,
A long, long way, away from him,
To the other side of the world.
Where the grass was green, year round.
She was lungless and wingless, but she did fly.
Boy, did she fly, so far away from him.

When his murmur of words died away,
Sitting with her back to the wall,
Her arms round her knees,
A conflict of emotions following one another
In quick succession across her face,
She said she had made up her mind, she was leaving,
Keeping her voice steady with an iron effort of will.

For a moment she thought he hadn't heard her.
He saw an almost painful sympathy in her eyes.
He looked at her, his eyes strangely impersonal.
With a long, exhausted sigh, he stood up,
His rage snapping. He picked up the whisky glass,
Took a couple of gulps from it and put it down.
Blood filmed his whisky eyes.
His expression changed to that of
Someone who had been struck in the face.

He simply stared, his eyes obsidian black,
And said, *go, if you have to, then go.*
His voice had sunk to a hiss.
He couldn't hide the sudden tremor in his voice.
If not for the whisky, he would
Have not made this mistake.

Part 2 – Monsoon of Kaveri

On My Acquaintances

Gopal Mama became a poet shortly after
Kaveri left him. They say that when one is
Deeply saddened in life, one becomes a poet.
Or a drunkard.
Gopal Mama became both.
With a pencil in his hand he felt real.
He felt almost like his father.
With a bottle in hand, he felt closer to Kaveri.
When he squinted through the amber rum,
He saw her there, smiling to him, her lips shimmering.

"The poet in me shakes hands occasionally
With my capering spirit, hushing it to its knee."
At times, they play the seesaw,
Rising and falling in my head."

"While one sleeps quietly,
The other walks the midnight beat.
While one dances down my spine on its turn,
The other stays awake, many a night,
Writing on me of justice and time."

"While one asks me where I'm going,
The other runs alongside,
Inhaling with rib-stretching gasps,
Its breath, a hurricane in my ears,
Imploring me to run with him

On the rattling train home from Wellore."

"And still, they shake hands, and make promises
That they would let the other have the other half of me,
Fighting like half-wives for room in my head"

The Taj's Poetry

Yadagiri said, "Speak to us on poetry"
And Gopal Mama replied,
"Poetry should be about two people making love
For the first time in their lives.
Poetry should be about feeling something for the first
And last time in a life, and letting those zealous lovers
Linger in a mind for a while, writing on it, as they would
On a soft bed, with their writhing.
Poetry is like childbirth without pain.
From the bowers of a gravid mind,
It should come quick and without much ado,
A delivery of thought that has long struggled for a voice or pen.
For, if laborious are the hands that write,
Painstaking are the eyes that read.
The difference is as subtle between good poetry and the passable
As that between a grandiose palace and the Taj.
While one was built for people's praise
The other was built out of true love and grief,
And hence is more remembered."

Pen, Paper and Ink

And the poet inside him spoke
While his alter ego slept,
Give me a pen. I'll lend
A voice to your pain.
And I'll make the paper
Out of the sinews of your heart.

I've been to places where
Seldom has trespassed a soul.
I, the poet in you, am one thing
But in the guise of another.
I am the sadness of a tortured
Wife dressed in the veil a smile.
I am the hesitant smile of a new bride
Hidden behind her guile,
Lest some elder takes her mirth
For a disallowed lack of shame.

I am this or that, but never myself.
I've seen the shower of your hot tears
Against the rainbows of your false smiles,
And I've known for long why
You have hidden your last tear.
For me to come along and use it to write with!

How I Became a Poet

The beginnings of anything is often
The most difficult thing to trace.
Where did this restless wind start
That rustles my shirt collar?
Where does the eternal, infinite ocean begin
That washes up on the shores of Vizag.
Where did language start?
How did I become a poet?
All loaded questions about beginnings
That you can only begin to answer.

I went to an Anglo-Indian school.
In eight grade, in letter-writing class,
I misspelled the word "Sincerely."
I think I missed an 'e.'
A heavy hand came down on my head,
A ton of bricks falling to earth.
I wrote a hundred times,
Sincerely, Sincerely, Sincerely…
Making sure of that last 'e,'
Which became magnified in my eye
Like a serpent head.

I would be in jail, today,
If I had not passed out of school.
Each time I saw his face,

My hands, transparent but potent,
Went out towards his ruddy neck.
Redneck.

In eleventh grade, I went to a
Christian Missionary College.
Once, when I *bunked* class and
Went to Liberty to watch a Hindi movie,
The vice-principal caught me.
He called me to his office.
Sitting behind the big oak desk,
His white father-tunic fading into
The white wall till only his angry face stood out,
His dark, hawkish face seeming
Never to have known a smile,
He asked me why I had committed this unspeakable crime.
There was a suspicious line at the corners of his mouth
I stammered something in my defense.
"Look at you, you can't even frame a sentence properly,"
He said with a sardonic expression.
Bloody uncivilized Indian villagers.
The last words did not come from his mouth
But I read them in the air,
Letters floating around, unframed.

I did learn to frame words,
Chaining them, one after another,
Like not-yet-bloomed jasmine flowers
That we brothers picked and strung together
In the garlands, which went
In our mother's hair.
My anger repelling their arrogance,
Creating sparks, creating conflict,
Giving birth to a rare sensibility to words.

The pen turned into an instrument of revenge.
That is how I became a poet.

Notes:
    Bunked: Indian slang for missing a class

Rhapsody of Birds and Cows

Yadagiri said, "What is true greatness?"
And Gopal Mama replied,
"Your greatness is not for you to speak.
It is he who will speak by your lips
Who placed it there in you with great care.
Greatness has no voice. It was born mute.
Let's just say all the greatness in you was spent before you were
born, in bringing you from an embryo to a recognizable form,
From squashed jelly to even a semblance of beauty.
It was placed in you before you learnt your first words.
It bloomed in you when you took your first steps.
And when you sang your first song to the saffron skies,
You were not alone, for many are the voices of greatness.
Greatness is not only in you but also all around.

The accustomed eye looks through greatness.
Where is the greatness in that shameless man, you ask,
The one who stands pissing on the street walls?
There is greatness in the workings of a life.
There is slight greatness in his bravery, too.
In his posture. In the heights he can reach.
In the very manner in which he has held
Half a litre of hot piss inside a balloon in his body,
Like a nine-month pregnant woman,
Getting ready to shoot twin babies out of her.
There is also greatness in the fact that the
Thing he holds in his hands is not only capable

Of excreting but also in giving new life.
There is greatness in that duality. Versatility.

There is a rhapsody in the air of birds and cows,
But it is you that wants to sing loudest,
Like a pompous peacock that unravels its wings amongst the fowl.
You fool, your greatness lies not in living in marble palaces
But building them with the sweat of your brow.
You'll realize you greatness when you sing
Along with those voices around you and not alone."

Footprint in the Sand

Yadagiri said, "And what of permanence"
And Gopal Mama replied,
"It is your biggest mistake, great fool,
That you build buildings of rock
With glass-paned windows,
Broken in a trice with the smallest of pebbles.
Like the decadent scorpion-shaped Falaknuma Palace,
Adorned with stained-glass windows
And multi-colored Venetian chandeliers.
Where is all its glory today?
Deserted by the Nizams who lived under its stingers
For bringing them ill luck.
You build sand castles up on the shore,
Strong and sturdy against the sea breeze,
Built with the precision of a jeweler, sand by sand.
You think the tides will revere its sides?
You think you have built something impregnable?
But it is no more permanent
Than an evanescent footprint in the sand.
The sea makes no disparity between the two,
An incidental, fleeting footprint and
A sand castle built with pain.
With one might swoosh, it takes everything,
Leaving nothing but lines of froth.
The only things that are permanent,
Within this rigid universe, are time and space,
And each entity occupies some space for some time.

Everything is accounted for, examined, weighed.
Like that castle that stands,
Presently, in front your watchful eye,
Is likely to wash up some distant shore at a later time."
Like Kaveri, who left him and reemerged in America.
"Everything dissolves in the ebb of time, is taken with it.
The sand came with the sea and
It'll return to where it belongs."

You

Yadagiri said, "speak to us on identity"
And Gopal Mama replied,
"Your identity is your trademark.
You were born with it.
It was stamped on your amorphous brow at conception.
Need you not expend any more wasteful sweat
In washing it off for uniqueness.
Your hunt for identity is like the mindless wind
That looks for notice in the eyes of the callous.
Those that know not that it exists,
And fear not its presence,
Till it finds its breath in the lungs of a tornado.
Knows it not that they were always applauding it,
Like the ovation of the rustling lurid leaves when it
Browsed its fingers through them.
Now, there are no spectators,
No leaves left on the once foliaceous, gnarled branches.
In finding its new identity,
It compromised on old friends,
Knows it not that to revere it, they need not fear it,
And sometimes, for the eyes to see,
The water has to cross over the nose."

The Worry Hanger

Yadagiri said, "Speak to us on riches"
And Gopal Mama replied,
"I envy not the wealthiest men.
They are capable only of prodigal sin.
My wealth lies elsewhere.
My wealth walks up to me
Each day, at some silent hour, when least expected
Takes my hands in its hands and
Leads me to the tide of its womanly hips,

Its breasts encircled with pearls,
Its skin caressed in sandalwood paste,
Its buttocks, round and curvaceous
As a rotund water-filled pot.
It smiles to me such a smile
That my eyelids scowl profanity at me
If sleep overcame me in its luminescence

When I came home each night
After long hours at work,
I removed all my worries off myself
And hung it up on her before retiring to bed.
When I left the next morning, I left without them.
For, I saw her beaming face in the morning light.
And that's where lies my Wealth."

Of Organs, Frogs and Bees

Yadagiri said, "Speak to us on perfection,"
And Gopal Mama replied,
"What else is more perfect to you
Than that that makes of you?
You deceive your rationale into
Hating every belief of the contrary,
Like an organ, engraved into your body,
Rejects all but that of the kith and the kin.

A frog in the well thinks no end
Of its world of perfection with a sky lit view.
Who can see the stars, and nothing else?
Better off is the bee that
Sucks off the pith of a flower.
Is he not free to roam the flowerbeds,
The hills, and the countrysides.

Which the frog and which the bee
Is for you to look into yourself, and see.
Look closely for exists there a thin line
Barring the gallant from the arrogant.
A costly mistake could this be if you did,
And chose either,
Would put you in the party of the latter.
Who could smell the flower, and nothing else?

DARK ROOMS

No one is perfect, Yadagiri.
We are all just prisoners of our own biases.
Our eyes can only look inward, into ourselves.
We are all prisoners of the dark rooms we live in."

God and Intelligence

Yadagiri said, "Speak to us on God,
About Intelligence," and Gopal Mama replied,
"God and Intelligence are two opposing forces.
It is not his intention that we be intelligent,
For then, we would be cleverer than him.
He is riddled with insecurities, too.

For this reason, in the heads of our ancestors,
Was a fear put of him. It is to these ancestors I was born,
Down a chain of ignorance. I was born out of this soil.
The same soil that runs in my blood, along with
Remnants of my ancestors who'd died in it.
The words they had writ in the grain, I hear still,
Long washed by countless rains.
They remain in every atom of me.
I know not their names. I do not know if they had any.
I know though that my lungs will lie mangled
In this very place, tread over by a million generations,
Who will not know my name, or that I manifested here,
Or that I exist, still!

They were ones whom I thank not
For pulling the tangible demons out of my head
And filling it with a bigger, untouchable fear.
For building a temple in my head.
For giving my thought a reason.
For defining fate, destiny and an almighty.

DARK ROOMS

Before, I fought demons in the open,
Trampling bison, man-eating lions, poisonous snakes,
I was not afraid. I did not know fear.
I burnt the breath of these demons with fire.
Today, I can compel the same fire to propel metal.
But I have no real demons to kill, just unreal gods.
Gods with metal vests I cannot penetrate.

I am more scared now.
Every newborn generation climbs the stair
Of intelligence. With each step, our fears gain
In magnitude, and the air thins.
Our fears today are owed to our intelligence.
I'm no cleverer than my predecessor,
Just that I started at a higher step, so I'm more afraid.
I'm afraid of heights, now, though I have overcome
The skies in rafts that sail the clouds.

I'm not any cleverer, I just take things for granted.
The fire that lights up, magically, by the
Strike of a match doesn't amaze me, anymore.
The fire burns coal, the coal boils water,
The water sublimes into vapor, and the vapor runs a train.
So what?
Am I missing something here? Did I lose a link somewhere?
All I see is the train—and I know it works.
We all know the theory, don't we?
What about the man who first struck rock to rock,
And transported the spark, painstakingly, to wood.
What about the man who built the first wheel.
Or the funny man who captured steam in a bucket
While having a bath, to move that wheel.
That's why I say I am not any cleverer,
I just assume too many things.

We now capture voice on plastic, today.
Haven't voices been trapped before in the
Echoes that ring back and forth in valleys.
We can now transport messages across lands,
But didn't we always. Just that
The very birds that carried the messages
Fall to the ground, burnt by wires
That carries people's voices.

God is the biggest demon.
I can't even eat without irking him.
I can eat plants but not a living being.
Now, I know plants live too,
But I can eat them. It's also in fashion.
Religion is god's tool to shape our minds.

The founder of religion was surely an environmentalist.
Religion started off and should have remained
The worship of nature's elements, physiolatry.
Geolatry, heliolatry, ignicolist astrolatry dendrolatry.
Rain, wind, earth, sun and water.
For without them, we'd not be here.
They were the rules we lived by. They were our demons.
Hence sprouted the gods that would fight them,
One god for each.
When man began to chain these demons,
Building canals and dams, these were not gods anymore.
The fury of the water was just like that of a hissing cat,
The sun became predictable. Its punctuality was its doom.
The earth could be ploughed to surrender.
The rains, like the sun, would come again.
Gods are born out of fear.
When this fear subsides, their end is near.

So, religion was bound to change.
Then came theriolatry, ophiolatry, litholatry, iconolatry.
Man gave god a form of his own self.
Man started building his own demons,
Something he could play with in his head.
Something so intangible that even today,
He hears voices, like a screwed-up schizophrenic,
That he cannot get rid off. Voices that say,
We're not demons, we're gods.
We'll be your caretakers when night comes.
We'll make sure to wake you up at dusk.
We'll be the ones to metamorphose you.
Like a beautiful butterfly that emerges from the
Body of a caterpillar, we'll send you back in new clothes.
Your present actions will be paid in the aftermath
And we, the accountants of your sin, will be watching.

They are demons, in reality, not gods.
And they live constantly, mostly in my head.

The body was separated from the thinking.
And all of a sudden, it was this car that needed fuel.
The fuel was named the soul.
Are we the only ones with souls?
Are we the only ones who have gods.
Can't you look inside an anthill and see
Their world, their temples, their altars.
There're creatures inside your eye,
Building a monastery on your lash,
That you can't see despite the proximity.
There are parasites inside you that are
Building churches out of you
Using your own blood and cells as mortar and brick.
Do they not have souls?
Do their souls have legs and hands too?

Some of them die in the wink of an eye,
Are all their souls around us, floating about.

The effect of religion is fanaticism.
The right to build illusions and facades,
And claims that ours is the only God.
We are the chosen people of a single heaven.
The rest are deemed children of a lesser God,
Many a sacrifice has been rent in his name,
Blood has been spilled across the face of history
And still the god-demons ride the world
And they live mostly in your head.

Platforms of Yesterday's Trains

I sat by the window seat in the Charminar Express,
Watching the platform outside.
A glowing kerosene lamp hissed from a bhajjia stand
On the platform. The coffeewalla yelled in his
Falsetto, "coffee, garama garam coffee"
The coolies—railway communists, walking-timetables,
The real lords of the stations, scurried from
Carriage to carriage, carrying heavy loads of luggage,
Their arms contained by their copper-brown armlets.
The huge clock on the wall lay still
In some other part of the day.
A coin-operated weighing machine blinked jazzily in the distance.
It told the weight and the future to varying degrees of accuracy.
What more could you get for fifty pice, these days.
Ting tong! A nasal voice that would put
Asha Bhonsle to shame announced in three languages,
"Madras bound Charminar Express
Will be leaving shortly from platform #7"
The stationmaster waved his green flag.
The engine driver waved back.
The platform turned in a panicky scene.
Latecomers started scurrying around,
Trying to find their carriages with their coolies.
The train started off with a lurch. I put my face against
The window and felt the hot air brush my face.
The soot from the engine entered my eye, bringing a tear

To my eye. Then, through my watery eyes,
I saw Poornima, outside on the platform,
Trying to get on the train.

Notes:
    Bhajjia: Indian side dish
    Garama Garam: Hot Hot
    Pice: Indian coin

Cocoon

I told Gopal Mama, one hot summer afternoon,
Sitting on the patio, that I would be
Going away to America, for further studies.
Gopal Mama looked at me, and said,
You are going to leave me, too?
Who will look after me?
I looked at him and he understood. He
Would have to look after himself.

"I don't want to know what life holds for me.
If I have to go, I will.
How I wish, to my inner self
Is obscured the fact of where my future lay.
To be in oblivion to the cocoon of my fate
That would one day burgeon into this world
As a dead worm, in the miscarriage of my dreams,
Or a veil of silk that would cover me with bliss!
Guard my child, my gravid surrogate. Whisper not the vaunts
Of where lies your land. Close yourself to glaring
Eyes, and curious ears, till it grows out
of your Cocoon.

Eye of the Crossroad

In the mere of my mind marches a dilemma of
An onerous loss for a blissful gain, I told Gopal Mama,
One day before I would be standing at the
The Chennai American Consulate for my visa,
The Consulate at Gemini Circle, Anna Salai.

"How can I leave these places,
These *chaat* stalls that have filled my evenings;
Mornings at the temples of my god, Shiva;
These double-decker buses that have
Staged the dramas of my love.
Can I leave all these and go away
To a brand new land on the other side.

Every moment of glory capers in an hour of truth.
Embarrassed by its amplitude.
Precocious of rejoicing early.
Every step of indulgence leads in a new direction
From the eye of the crossroads,

Crossroads where those very buses,
Bent to the ground, careen, where I stand bemused,
Hoping to find a cerebral navigation,
To a land of discovery, or my way back
To the possessions of a past."

   Notes:
      chaat: Indian side dish

A Boat on my Hand

To this, Gopal Mama said, "Followed have I
All my life the lines across the fore of my palm,
Scribbled there for posterity, at birth."

"Made time a river and watched its flow by the lands.
And time, my alter ego, watched me walk those lines,
Bemused, but not cynical of what I could be
One day, I'll reach the sea, and I'll watch you
Walk right off the edge, it whispered, so I didn't hear,
Unless you go with me!"

"The pull of a river that runs over shallow rocks
Is too strong to resist. It has turned rock to pebbles,
It will do the same with you if you resist. Soften. Ground.
It knows how to cut your corners, wilt your will.
You have to be like the weed that flows with it,
Shy and deceiving,
You will pretend you want to go with the river.
And go, you have to, dear nephew, he said,
A new land calls you, as a lighthouse beckons the ships.
Time will stop for me, but it will not for you."
You have to go, he said with a tear in his eye.

Part 3 – Summer of Kaveri

Not a Sound to Hear

One year later, Gopal Mama asked me
What I felt about America. I wrote back,

"Not a sound to hear, only the calm to fear,
I stand up at the pier, and look to the water's mere,
Days that promptly die, and mornings numbered by my
Clean underwear and unfelled hair."

"Counting the cerebrations of my brain
That keeps coming the grain, these windless afternoons,
I refrain from causing my forces to drain;
Not a sound to hear, only the calm to fear."

So, even you fear the calm, he wrote back, laughing,
I could almost see a look of veiled amusement
Cross his face for a split second as he wrote those words.
I thought something was wrong with these dark rooms.
When night comes, dark and disguised in the veil of Kaveri,
I can hear the cockroaches screwing under the mattress,
The sound of lizards clicking tongues on the walls
Fills me with the thought, am I the only one without a mate.
Am I the only one in the world left heirless.

I told him that I bumped into Kaveri.
Of course, you don't bump into
Someone in this huge country, America.
I did not tell him that I went to see her.

She called me for lunch. I met her kids.
She is happy, I wrote.

He wrote back saying he hears her making love
To her new man. They come in little packets of grief.
Her moans of ecstasy ring in his ears, traveling across oceans
Like a handclap at the gates of Golconda Fort
Is heard at the highest *durbar* of the Fort.

Notes:
    durbar: gallery

You Are the Country

In one of my letters to Gopal Mama,
I wrote to him of how much I missed my country.
The air, full of pollution and
The cries of a nation of people,
The water, with all its diseases,
Yet tasty as the tamarind-flavored pani *puri,*
The cold breeze against a soaking shirt
After a sudden monsoon spell comes and
Turns the roads into little rivers.
Rivers we run splashing through,
Uncaring of colds and coughs,
The cocoa-colored water filled
With the fresh smell of earth.
The fires, which seem to glow brighter, there.
Brahma's pink lotus, Vishnu's serpent, Shiva's Ganga.
Clay Lord Ganesha idols floating in the river, Laxmi and Saraswati,
The wonderful comic books of the
Ramayan, Mahabharat and the Puranas,
Sunflower-yellow *ladoos* and *jilebis,*
Soft white *idlis* that melt in the mouth,
Trains that come and go
Stations, *coolies* and crossings,
Baby rockets of Deepavali in the skies
The colors of *holi* in the air, on the streets,
On the faces of people who lose their shyness,
Amar Akbar Anthony, Sholay, Bobby,
The happy-sad voice of Kishore,

The uplift of *bhangra* and *dandia*,
The elegance of *kathak, kuchipudi, bharatnatyam*,
The scare in the *kathakkali*,
The heartbeat of the *tublas* and *mrugangams*
The sadness in the *veenas* and *sitars*,
The rare sun at Ooti, Darjeeling, Shimla and Musoorie,
Musical crows on power-lines,
Jittery sparrows bathing in little, limpid pools,
Territorial dogs strolling in gangs,
Adamant cows refusing to budge,
Corruption, disease, poverty and filth,
All its languages and faces,
Smiles, Smiles, Smiles.
I stand on top of this pile of words
Knowing it is just the tip of an iceberg.

Notes:
    puri: Indian side-dish made of wheat
    Ganga: the Ganges River, believed to emanate from Shiva's head
    Ganesha: Elephant-headed Indian god. After Ganesh Chaturti, a festival dedicated to Lord Ganesha, his statues are left to melt away in rivers and lakes.
    Laxmi: The consort of Lord Vishnu.
    Saraswati: Goddess of Knowledge.
    Ramayan Mahabharat Puranas: Ancient Indian epics
    ladoos, jilebis: Indian sweetmeats
    idlis: native Indian rice cakes
    coolies: Railway porters
    Amar Akbar Anthony, Sholay, Bobby: names of Indian movies
    bhangra , dandia: Traditional Indian folk dance
    kathak, kuchipudi, bharatnatyam, kathakkali: Classical Indian dance forms
    Ooti, Darjeeling, Shimla and Musoorie: Indian hill resorts

The Country is in You

What makes a country a country?
"Your country is not where you have stood,"
And Gopal Mama replied,
"Nor is it where you stand now.
It is not in such a shallow place as to be
Trampled by a billion filthy feet.
It is in a much deeper place, well beyond soles and spit.
It is not what you behold around you.
Your country is not exposed in your eyes
But hidden in a deeper throbbing kingdom,
In an abysmal pit where eyes cannot pry.
It is not the sand and the dirt in the air.
These are things you learn to leave behind
But you still take your country with you.

It is in the songs you sing to the morning air.
It is in the gods that have gone with you,
Following the soft whispers of your prayers.
Like the migrant bird that always flies back
When the season to go home is signaled on the horizon
By the first rays of sun that come to thaw the rivers,
You learn to walk back within your heart to your country.

It is not you that lives in your country,
It is the country that lives in you.
For without the souls littered of you and your kindred,

A land is but a land and the air is but air
It is you who have made your country a country."

The Clock

I left my love behind in India. Poornima,
Along with all the smells that twitch the nose,
All the sights that make you cry,
And all the colors that flutter your heart.
These, I failed to put away in a suitcase,
At least not within baggage limit
Even though they were weightless, really
I took with me only the ugly heavy things.
I wished I could take her eye, a strand of her
Shikakai smelling hair, long and brown,
A corner of her lip. An ear lobe, with her earring.
I only managed to pack in a big heavy
Picture of her, frame included.

She would be with me, one day.
I knew she would wait. And I would wait for her
As Gopal Mama has waited for Kaveri.

I wrote to her, one day, about how much I missed her,
How I wait to be with her. Counting clock ticks.
"These skinny, shiny roads run endlessly from
The center of my brain, crisscrossing labyrinths
That takes me no place. I lose myself amongst the
Dense throngs in the bazaars and marketplaces
Where vegetable vendors hold up ripe-purple
Eggplants in my face.

I hurry myself over them, roads that have
Survived the writing of centuries
Of feet over them, and the Moghuls. And the Raj.
Roads that never seemed to reach their promised lands,
Their destinations.
I hurry to realize my promise of punctuality,
To make my rendezvous with time.
I scarce know of my tryst with you.
I am wholly in your two hands. You are my clock...

Notes:
    Shikakai: a herbal shampoo

A Lover's Recipe

Then I wrote to Gopal Mama, asking him
To speak to me of love.
What is it that you felt for Kaveri
That has made you wait all these years?
Gopal Mama replied, "You think you are in love
But you are in love with yourself.

You think that you have found love
Because you have a recipe in hand and
The ingredients you wish in her.
But tell me this, which recipe can better the
Cooking of a mother who toils over
A pot of *baingan bartha* with just her love.
The only recipe that works is the recipe of god.
Love is made in heaven, not on hand-written recipes.

You need the shadow of a sycophant
That praises you and loves you.
A shadow that dances with you
But never crosses your step.
You want it to be attached always to your body.
You shield it from the sun, its origin,
The same sun that owns it, really.
If some straying hand that grasps for it
Should only find it thin into air."

Gopal Mama believed that the only true love
In the world was his love.

"And when the incandescent carnal fires in
Your heart leap up like muscled tongues,
You want the silhouette to metamorphose
Into a statuesque damsel in your hand,
Unknowing that there are boundaries
To be crossed between love and intimacy,
But boundaries that should be walked across,
Not jumped over.
There are walls in between that need to be climbed,
But not that should be leaped over.
For he who leaps will find many such walls,
With dry lands in between,
Moments of pure ecstasy but never lasting solace.
And he who climbs will falter for years to the top.
He sees vast fields of flowers
To where the eye meets the sky."

Notes:
    baingan bartha : an Indian dish made out of eggplant

Scaring Yama

One day, my friends pulled me
To an Indian classical-music concert
Despite my complaints that I was
Not much of a *classical music* person.
No one is born a *classical music* person.
No one is born to the soft wind of a flute
Or the dreamy strumming of a *tanpura,* they said,
One is born to the music of one's own
Heart-wrenching cries from the lack of air,
Lungs filled with putrid, womb-air.
One has to go, sit and breathe
Culture and music into one's veins.
One has to become immune to the
Boredom that comes unasked with it.
It's like on going back to India, you
Have to breathe its air into your lungs
To accustom yourself, again,
To the "ias"—bacteria, malaria, pneumonia
To the "tions"—corruption, population and speculation
To the "tys"—poverty, spirituality and diversity.
(I did not know that a country
Could be summed up in handful of suffixes)

That is the way it is done.
One has to sterilize oneself
From the oncoming sahib-sickness.
Why, you have been here one year,

In this blasted cultureless country
And you have already become a sahib.
There is no hope for you.
You will settle down here, get married,
Have three NRI kids and die
A lonely, painful death, surrounded by
Nothing but the quietness of death.

This is the only country in the world
So quiet, you will hear *Yama's*
Measured footsteps, even when he tiptoes,
Coming to your bed with his snorting buffalo.
Then, you will need this classical music.
Yama hates it.
Not much of a classical music person, either.
For it comes from the chords of God.

Notes:
    NRI: Non-Resident Indian
    Yama: Lord of death
    tanpura: Traditional Indian string instrument

A Knife in the Throat

So, I went, sat and listened.
Raagam, taanam, pallavi.
I closed my eyes, trying to force
Myself to listen to the music.
The brown, spiced voice began to sing.
I tried to breathe in the music.
I learned one thing that day,
That you cannot breathe music
Just like you cannot see smells,
The smells of the *chaat* stalls back home,
Just like you cannot taste a wondrous sight,
The sight of *holi* colors in the air.
You can only grasp for it with
One desperate hand with the hope of
Catching something in your hands.

Now, I only half listen as
I struggle with my conscience,
Deep in formless thought.
I feel alive with meaning, alive in every fiber.
I try to listen to the sirens of the trains
At Kachiguda station. All I hear is shrill
Wail of a woman who must
Have just lost her husband.
Like Nusrat Fateh Ali's voice that climbs
Higher and higher with each note,
As though he was poised between life and death,

Trying to reach the ears of
A lover from a previous birth.
A pulse beating and swelling at the base of his throat
As though his heart had risen from its usual place.

You cannot try to find your country
In high-pitched voice of a singer
Who wails away to the evening air
Like a knife were stuck in his throat,
Like his vocal chords were about to burst
Open in a splash of blood.
Or the drummer beating his fingers
On the two-headed *mrudangam*,
Following the beat of his heart.
You can only make a request.

Notes:
    Raagam, taanum, pallavi: pieces of a classical Carnatic music composition.

Beacon in the Wind

My mother often asked me, in her long letters
That made their way across oceans to me,
Still bearing her breath and the smell of fresh
Aricanut she washed her hair with each Saturday.
"Don't you feel bored, all alone, in that alien country,"

And I said almost instinctively,
"I'm never bored, mother. I live mostly in my head.
My thoughts are my best friends.
In them, I'm in love with a different
Woman each day. Each day is a new season.
Now, I'm traveling light years in space.
Some distant star beckons me often.

There are cerulean seas all around, cajoling
Its child in its bouncing lap,
Like that mother whose breath is everywhere.
Her voice beckons me often,
And I go to her each day, in my thoughts.
I'm never bored! I live mostly in my head."

Notes:
  aricanut: a seed used as a shampoo

My Mother's Sweat

How much I missed the smell of
Her warm perspiration,
Became the topic of one of my letters to her.
The smell of fresh coconut water,
In this land where the smell of people,
Sweat and pheromones, god-given perfumes,
Is dissolved away in antiperspirants.

"I have breathed memories of you in
Every trickle of your warm perspiration.
Rich rewards of your travails over
The smoking *unoon*.
Your smells, mixed with the scent
From the ends of your hair,
Wet with water juiced with *aricanut* seed,
The *attar* on your steamy body
Fragrant with a pinch of spices,
My nose swoons from overwork at the thought.

Starts its journey where of.
From your musk-laden armpits,
Where you carried me, a body-clinging child.
Each smell carries a memory.
And each memory is strung to other memories.
Each drop takes me to a new place.
Now, I am sitting on your lap, covered
In your peacock-pattern pallu,

The smell of ivory mothballs in my nose.
Now I am being knuckled on my head
For kissing your face so hard my teeth have left
Impressions on your copper-fair skin.

Now, you have become modern.
You have *ponds dreamflower* talcum power,
That prevents my dreams from flowering.
Now your sweat trickles into a bed of talc,
To be cremated with the stagnant creation
Of a moschiferous goat's gland.

Now, you are miles away,
Smell carries only so far.
Three years of blanched anticipation
To smell it on you, that which I have lost.
Mother, it's not the heart that has forgotten,
It's the nose.

Notes:
    unoon: a furnace

The Mind's Impressionism

Three years passed. Poornima waited
For me, and I waited for her.
She, as faithful as Sita.
Me, I was Ram during the thirteen-year exile.

I wrote to her, "I close my eyes,
Find you on the back of my eyelids,
Etched there, for posterity, in a visage of color,
An unfound masterpiece
Splashed across the retina of my brain.
Here, every aesthetic eye of a distant memoir
Stands admiring this release
From my helpless intangibility,
As a connosouier stands admiring
The impressionism of Monet,
Feeling the movement of a scene
That has become frozen in time,
In repose, not as beautiful,
But in animation, astonishing.

I see you in the bazaar, wearing a *ghagra*
Embroidered with magenta peacocks of thread,
And a *choli,* glinting with mirror work in the sun.
I watch you from the window of my bus,
The vision of you is silent impressionism on my eye.
The bus moves on, yet your smile lingers,

Reminding, yet not assuring of your permanence.
When my eyes flutter open, you vanish from me.
The maze of colors that ripples before my eyes is gone

Notes:
    ghagra: Indian skirt
    choli: Indian blouse

Will Work for Food

Gopal Mama wanted to know if really
All people in America were happy. He had heard
That from someone, from some idiot who had never been
To the States.
Someone told him and he believed it?

Gopal Mama could not believe that
There existed such a place outside of his dark rooms.

I told him I saw something the other day.
"Will work for food. One man stood with his woman,
Two little boys and a girl,
With a sign at the entrance to the Mall.
The youngest clung onto to his mother's breast,
A tear in his eye. An empty stomach will
Bring him new nightmares in the night.
The older ones were brave and clung tight to their father.

I went back much later to see if I could find them there.
They were not there, where I'd seen them,
They'd found work, I thought,
I returned home and had my dinner."

There is sadness and helplessness everywhere.
You will have to learn to work your way out of it.
He wrote back asking when his little nephew started
Teaching him how to live.

You have grown up so fast, he wrote.
I head his laughter burning black holes in the aerogramme.

The Bride Making

In the summer of 2001,
Poornima became a bride, my bride.
Now, quietly, she watches as holy-gray ash
Is smeared across her uninitiated,
Unblessed forehead, castigating it for life!

A tiny temple is built around her brow,
Bringing Gods to her young mind
That is only yet opening itself
To the devils of new found youth;
Incarcerating it into a world of her
Impending womanhood that is only slightly
emphasized by the tiny swell of her heaving breast.

She watches this temple melt down her cheeks,
Washed in her happy-sad tears,
As a new god, her hairy man
Walks in through those eyes,
Ringing the bells as he enters.
Seven doors fling open, unchecked to him,
Those she has carefully locked all her life
To men, wolves and sin.

The very doors that have shielded her soul,
Her breast and her love—
Are flung open to his leaden footsteps.

Steps that enter stealthily—sprayed
With flowers in each step. Now, she tells herself,
He is my god, I am his slave. I am a bride at last!

The Bridegroom Making

So many grains of yellow turmeric,
Tainted with vermilion rice, have I ever
Held in all my life—in my head?
More than the hair that cradles them,
More than all the memories
That lay within—grains of time.

My hands, rubbed by women
I barely know, with jaundiced paste,
Provoking my male pride,
And bringing unknown shame
To my face that quivers under
The eyes of all those aunts—
Aunts that wait their turn to rub.

Then, the head-aunt pours water
From the dimpled steel bucket
Over my oiled head,
Cleansing the tainted rice
To the white tile,
The yellow of it spreading like
The vapor of moonlit fog.
She rubs my ears and nose
Squeaky clean, like I was a baby,
While other aunts watch, laugh.

Then they say in unison,
Now you are a Bridegroom.
Now you are a bridegroom at last!

The Reopening of a Diary

Today, I decided my life
Was worth recording, again,
In a diary, ten years after I penned
My last year in a tan-bound.
Yes, I have gone through
That adolescent disillusionment,
Where I felt my life slip away
Into the meaninglessness of youth,
Of building a life I did not want.
That was when I stopped and closed it,
Never thinking I would
open it again in this lifetime.

Now I think twice.
My hands shudder at the implications.
I am a bridegroom, now!
Is there reason in my life now?
Is there going to be happiness alone
That I will look back in ten years
Or would I be closing this again?

The Mother-In-Law Making

Hesitant is her stare back.
Her face contorted with jealousy and anger,
Is her son by her side? The new bridegroom.
She is afraid, as is told by her heart
That fluttered wildly in her breast,
To find him not there, but with his
New bride—the new apple of his eye.

The bride's arm Resting on his shoulder,
Where she hoped she would
Find a place. He sees her searching glances,
Filled with secret disappointment,
And hurries to her side, leaving his bride for her,
A satisfied light comes into his eyes.
He lingers by her side, his heart in a tug of war
Between old love and new passion—between
Aging, menopausal tantrum
And the freshness of his bride's hair.

She says with a tear in her eye,
Now you will forget me,
More a tiresome question
Than a statement or an order,
A realization of the removal of
The can'ts, won'ts and don'ts
From her vocabulary,

At least when it came to him,
Now you are a bridegroom, she says
Now I am a mother-in-law at last.

The Child Marriage

In amusement, we all watched; a smirk
On the lips of the elders
But laughter inside all of us.
The three-year-old bridesmaid,
Mock married to her young cousin,
As they playfully, mischievously
Exchanged the garlands that
Were meant for the older weds.

A young photographer stood
Poised to click a picture,
His fingers framing the infant couple.
They did not need to be told to smile,
These came easy to them.
Unlike shame and shyness!
The bride giggling, bold,
The fake bridegroom, holding
His bride without any shame.

The other children throwing
Rice blessings and yelling,
Wait there is more to be done
Before this marriage is done,
As their mothers shout to them
To stop, to behave—but only
To placate the elders.
But none wanted this to stop.

Deep down, they wanted this
Innocent ceremony to bring back
Their very own naïve days,
To take them back to all that innocence,
Which they lost at the altars or god,
And the phalluses of their men.

Poornima

Poornima was carrying our first baby
When I decided to name the child
Poornima, after her mother.
Don't ask me how I was going to
Avoid the confusion of calling the one and
Having the other reply, when words would
Be put, inevitably, on the lips of little Poornima.

In Sanskrit, Poornima means 'full moon.'
"One full moon cradling a half-moon,"
I would sing to the unborn Poornima,
"Little one, you're still the forming
Of a dream, awaiting a release
From the bloody uterus of my brain."

"A figment of silver imagination
Stirring in my gravid conscience.
A stilled sculpture in my mind,
Without eyelids or irises or legs or hands,
Awaiting reincarnation. Amorphous. Lifeless,
Yet shapely as your mother's abdomen.
Neatly packaged and self-contained as an egg,
Ugly, screwing your tiny face into a thoughtful,
Wizened caricature in your sleep,
Buried in the shadow lands of thought,
You make me live through the travails of everyday,
As I look to the light when you burgeon

From the tomb of the present
To take birth in the womb of the future."

The Dollar Seven Coats

My parents visited me in America.
They came for the arrival of little Poornima.

I bought my father these dollar seven coats,
Russet, two of them, at Burlington Coat Factory.
He looked at me with a question in his eyes,
"Have I done enough for you to buy me these?"
Seven dollars, fourteen for both!

And he justified their worth in their praise,
Giving vent to his guilt for making me buy them.
And I looked at his glorious burnet eyes.
Something flickered far back in them.
And asked, "are you really asking me this?"

For the man who wore the coat of life on me
With just a trickle of his blood.
And on many a rainy day, took off his coat
And placed it over my head, while he drenched.
To getting me into a graduation suit
With many long years of his sweat,

I wondered how many of those coats,
Dollar seven coats, I would need to buy him
Before I repaid all the coats he'd bought me.
He looked in my eyes and I hoped he knew.

The Passing of a Dream

An army is coming marching
Down the gray-white spine.
They pass on without stopping, Yama's men.
A thousand hoofs bludgeoning under them
A dream, still struggling for life
In a blanched, expectant womb.

The tread of feet, a dolorous lullaby,
No, a mournful dirge, puts the dream-child to rest,
The soles squish as though trampling a ripe-red tomato,
And it feels little pain as they pass over.

Little Poornima did not make it.
The full moon was eclipsed.

Notes:
    Yama: Lord of Death. Keeper of Hell.

Kaleidoscopes

Here, in this cruel world
Of 'expression kaleidoscopes,'
Of smiles, frowns, smirks, and stares,
Where a smile is a sadness
That you hide behind its veil,
Or conceal behind a hand.
Where to be solemn, an inadequacy of mirth,
My lips quaver in this moment of indecision,
At the crossroads where
A smile meets a tragedy,
People watching me through
Those colored Kaleidoscopes,
My head ringing like a Chinese gong,
Tossed into a dilemma,
Whether to cry or remain strong.
My lips shake as the news of
Little Poornima comes to me

Notes:
    Yama: Lord of Death. Keeper of Hell.

Playing Yama

At my doorstep, I saw a slimy little conchiferous snail
Making its way to the center of my walkway
Like a village belle walking to the well,
Swaying her hips, a pot on her head.

Its watery footsteps, a trail of blobs,
Traces its slow, painstaking path.
I step over it, not wanting to hurt it.
How long did fate plan this for me,
Making me forget of the snail, on my return,
Framing me, conning me into unknown sin.
Nine hours for that snail to crawl under my foot,
Like Poornima, who crawled for
Nine jailed months towards oblivion.

As though it was born for that single cause
Of disturbing the karma of my next lives
By making me a killer in this.
When I heard the crunch under my foot
I felt a life leave its body and spiral up my spine.
Did Yama feel the same sensation
When he trampled over my Poornima.

The Well

"Mother do you have a tear left for me,"
I remember asking her that day
When she cried all day, huge teardrops
Trickling down the wings of her nose
Till she had none left in the buckets of her eye.
She cried for little Poornima.
Little Poornima died without seeing the world.

"Look to the bottom of the well
And you'll find a solitary drop, all alone."
I looked into that well and was dismayed,
For the well had dried to a crisp.

The water exhausted by village belles that came
To fetch water in their pots. I felt my enthusiasm fade
But then I heard my mother's familiar lisp,
"Will you tell me—is it the last drop
Or is it the well beginning to fill!"
She blinked back the sudden scalding tears

Tear in the Quarry

Poornima would not speak for months.
I would whisper to her, trying to
Bring her out of her coma.
"Go on, cry. Don't you feel anything?"
With a great false show of indignation
Only to realize her sense of loss was beyond tears.
It was visible in her vacant pink-rimmed eyes.
"A patch of land, sublime stretch of your face,
I stooped to sow, forever my sorrow,
To reap a tender smile, to keep."

"The heart has scorched to a sinewy quarry
Of glinting stone, alter ego of your moonstone face.
Cast in it a trickle of water,
Has awaited many a blanched year
In its shallow grave of metamorphic
To turn into a river and fill that quarry."
Only the strange hotness on her cheeks
Told me that she was crying when
Her eyes burst open, at last, like dam.
She bit off a hysterical laugh

Kaveri's Last Summer

At the same time as the demise
Of little Poornima, I received news of Kaveri.
She was killed in a car crash in Iowa.
In her heart she had always been afraid
Of being crushed between metal.
It was her fate, I guess.

Gopal Mama read the news, my short
Three-word letter written to him, "She is dead,"
With silent denial, at first.
He scanned the closely written lines
To find some hidden prank in their midst.
His heart refused to believe his mind
Though his mouth felt like old paper, dry and dusty.
The remembrance he felt startled him.
He put the letter down but his eyes still rested
On the afterimage of the text.

She would be back after the monsoons.
It was summer, still, and the Kaveri does
Dry up in summer, he denied his fears.
After the monsoons came and went,
He realized he had lost her, forever.
His face turned to a mask as cold as a funeral.
A look of disbelief, rage and frustration.
He tried to swallow the sudden bile
That had risen in his throat.

He realized he had lost, just like all his siblings, though
His loss had come slow and painstakingly.
He had believed, just like all of them,
That if he stood tall and proud,
Like his father stood in the framed photograph,
Kaveri would return to him one fine day,
Beg for his forgiveness, and fall at his feet.
And he would pardon her.
To forgive, to dismiss, was a rare power they all held
But never got a chance to exercise.

He clenched his jaw to kill the sob in his throat
And ended up weeping with great shuddering sighs.
His breath came in quick shallow gasps.
His lungs inhaled in long priapic pants
Trying to control the panic that
Was threatening to overtake him.

"Inevitable as Love was at the start,
Oh! We believed in "death do us part."
Like we believed in the Sanskrit prayers
We read each morning to gods without ears.
Still, one day, we knew we had to part.
I let you sink out of this weeping heart.
Into the inky blue of the death hour,
Forever my mind's eye shall scour,
The ocean bottoms; in every star;
On my skin; in my hair,
In the blackness, to find you there."

The first poem he wrote that rhymed.
He felt Kaveri deserved it.

Stopping by Tank Bund

For the first time in years, Gopal Mama stepped out
Of his dark rooms. He locked the house,
Opened the huge gate with
The iron-bolt and went to Tank Bund.
He walked with the slouch of a frequenter of taverns,
The sharp, sweet-sour smell of sooty
Hyderabad air filled his nostrils, quickly.
How difficult it must be to walk
With a knife in one's heart.

He stopped by at the bridge to look at the boats,
Sailing happily below clean-cut white clouds.
How the world has changed, he thought,
Everything is so fast, everybody going somewhere.
Coming back to the same place.
They have even built this huge granite
Statue of the Bodhisattva right in the middle
Of the Hussain Sagar.

He looked longingly over his shoulder.
"I turn back; I can feel your presence.
The wind has pushed your hair back.

I can see you looking over my shoulders
At the waters below."
A hand descended on his shoulder from behind.
He felt the silky weight of Kaveri's hair slide onto his face and neck

"I can see your face on them,
I can see you flowing there, going someplace far away.

Did you not like to flow? I wish I had gone with you.
I was stupid to think paper boats did not have banks.
I should have known, where one bank meets the other,
That was where I would get off.

Makes me wonder about those boats, will they stop for me?
Will the water freeze in my vision for just a moment,
Like I have stopped at this bridge.

He saw a boat pass by, the boatman's oar dipping
In and out, the sound of a pebble dropping in puddle,
As silent as a raindrop that falls off the gate.

He sees Kaveri, her feet drifting along on a cloud.
He seizes her invisible hands from the winds,
Enfolding them in his own.
He holds them pressed against his chest

In his vision, the boat climbs up the bank,
Slides onto the slippery bark of a palm tree that lay bent in the water.
Slowly, it climbs, disappearing into the
Fountain of branches at the top, into the sunshine.
A satanic smile spreads across his thin lips.
He laughs, a humorless vicious sound.
Featherlike laugh lines crinkle around his eyes.
The earth falls away and he goes with her to
That place of rapture, utterly consumed,
Thinking he saw her smiling face there.

The next day, Gopal Mama was found, face down in the
Slush, his lungs full of Moosi's sewage.